# UNDISCLOSED

# PREVIOUS BOOKS BY RUTH O'CALLAGHAN

*Poetry*

*Double Binary,* Shoestring Press 2022
*A Rickle Of Bones,* Shoestring Press 2020
*Unportioned,* Salmon Poetry 2019
*Mapping the Light,* Shoestring Press 2018
*Wringing Blood,* Salmon Poetry 2018
*Vortices,* Shoestring Press 2016
*An Unfinished Sufficiency,* Salmon Poetry 2015
*The Silence Unheard,* Shoestring Press 2013
*Another Morning of Quiet Pleasures,* Soaring Penguin Press 2013
*Goater's Alley,* Shoestring Press 2010
*A Lope of Time,* Shoestring Press 2009
*Where Acid Has Etched,* bluechrome 2007


*Other publications*

*Without Skin: Interviews with 23 Internationally Renowned Women Poets,*
    Soaring Penguin 2016
*Un Salt in Timp (A Lope of Time),* Universității din București 2012
*Echoes From The Steppe: An Anthology of Contemporary Mongolian Women's
    Poetry,* Edited by Ruth O'Callaghan, Soaring Penguin Press 2011


*C.D.s*

*Echoes From The Steppe,* 2011
*And The Story So Far,* 2009

# UNDISCLOSED

## RUTH O'CALLAGHAN

Shoestring Press

Printed by imprintdigital
Upton Pyne, Exeter
www.digital.imprint.co.uk

Typesetting and cover design by The Book Typesetters
hello@thebooktypesetters.com
07422 598 168
www.thebooktypesetters.com

Published by Shoestring Press
19 Devonshire Avenue, Beeston, Nottingham, NG9 1BS
(0115) 925 1827
www.shoestringpress.co.uk

First published 2023
© Copyright: Ruth O'Callaghan
© Cover photograph: Roof of St John the Baptist, Bishop's Castle, Shropshire by Clare Brant

The moral right of the author has been asserted.

ISBN 978-1-915553-40-9

# CONTENTS

IV

I

# SHADES

There is no-one left who remembers that winter.
Wind wound garments tight, each pore shrank
into itself, skin was simply the body's shroud.

A crippled angel hungered for festive light
in Trinity's cemetery, the priest inexplicably
absent though the dog had been brought inside.

Now I know there is no let from those annexed days
and who is there willing to hear the dead words
of the living living through words of the dead? –

so they remain unburied, unhurried as in life.
The hands of the clock crucify time. Distance
is not measured in metres, it is in the laying out

of lives after the last sputter of breath, the last myth
laid to rest. It was that winter pipes rusted
our water, salvaged, twice boiled

as if life could be filtered, the rim of memory
dredged to encompass all: but only death allows
such provision. Listen! There will be no contradiction!

# PRELUDE

Night-lit the street becomes harbinger.
    Margins dissolve.
A rat creases into a same-self-grey wall

waits while a fox slinks alone
    along
     a long corridor of bins

today's detritus
      removal imminent.
Windows wink out light and then wink-out light

leaving dark to discover the harsh cry of desire
unveil the wanton
     which mingles with the child's wail
when wall-shadow stoops to *cwtsh* her
in the absence of her absent mother.

The body in the bag humps, stiff with cold
knows the import each sound declares
knows absence
    desire
      absence of desire
but desires warmth's absence.
Tonight, the prod of a cop's boot must suffice

as must the nurse's fingers seeking your vein
the drip that ekes blood
the catheter draining urine
     the susurration of skirt
in a night-lit corridor where hurrying footsteps are harbinger

Tonight the fox will not scream
     nor will you hear
rails rattle under trains
    drilling
    through the seam of night

their load of nuclear waste (bound
                              in pristine steel drums)

                              sufficiently decayed
to be efficiently moved through suburbs.
Efficient, too, your move
                    bed-bound
                    toward another station
where an arch-browed matron awaits departure.

Today I've moved limbs
                 skimmed flecks of butterfly-dry
                              spittle from lips
that read me endless texts
        imprisoned in Victorian tapestries.
You did not wake. The gape of mouth slack.

Unbuttoned
             your throat lies open to the dark.
The dark where you lie cannot be punctured.

Your dirty gowns have been gathered
                              binned
today's detritus          removal imminent.

The orderly forgets fresh.          Harbinger.

# ATROPHY

While minutes and hours drain away
a foxy sun fades in the dying year,
each day discarded marks its prey.

What remains may soon decay
ambitions fail, friends disappear
while minutes and hours drain away

and days become a drear display
with all direction still unclear.
Each day discarded marks its prey

even as children run, laugh, play,
explore this avenue, that frontier,
while minutes and hours drain away.

Consider your options but stay
aware, shadows draw ever-near:
each day discarded marks its prey.

You cannot delay time. Try to defray
simply exposes an underside of fear
as minutes and hours drain away:
each day discarded marks its prey

## ON EXAMINATION

How do we know what lies beneath?
Will it groan when a roughshod foot
cracks a twig or a barrow furrows fresh-wet

soil ploughing the narrow path
between mounds that barely disguise....
Best not go there. But as each jolt tips the load

over the just dead
– are there any just dead?
How do we know what lies beneath?

# ON REFLECTION

This is the rag and bones of it.
The last flutter of our flag flying
at half mast, our glass less than
half, drained, only sediment left: but what remains, savour: love.

II

# REHEARSAL

The Director hoarded the script, ensconced
– and that truly is the only word for it: *italicised*
when in print or, if uttered, with rising inflexion,
a somewhat higher register but with definite
emphasis and with, perhaps…no, definitely,
a twist of lips – but maybe that's a riff too far?
Ensconced on his throne, minions fluttering
feathers as his actors are despatched, untested, onto a stage to build a
performance without guidance:
                              *Improvisation, darlings! Be dominant!*

                                         *


What did the parents say? They were parents.
Well, eventually. But when it kicked off – zilch.
Two kids left to range around, aimless.
Paradise unleashed, little constriction.
No wonder the one restriction was broken.
Youth has to test its metal, stamp its mark
or whatever cliche you prefer…….. It didn't seem much.
In my day we called it scrumping. If caught, a quick clip.
Not that hullaballoo. Butch Featherman! Flaming sword!
                              Such over-reaction even for Him.

# ACTS

For surely that's from where we all stem/return.
                Nothing is linear.
Your hands gracing a book that holds Genesis
                bear witness.
Their curve clasps the cover of the family Bible
                eyes scan
creation: paradise, freely given but knowledge
                – where dominance lies –
retained by the benefactor. Nothing is linear.
                Random disruption
refuses to recognise the usual conventions.
                Perfect balance
between heaven/earth is overthrown, the fulcrum
                dislocated
temporarily it is true but consequent apocalypse
                pursues
and so the simple act of eating an apple removes
                harmony, amasses
armies: a cold wind sweeps from the Caucuses
                varies vertically
horizontally, according to elevation, latitude and location.
                Nothing is linear.
                Bridges are needed.

\*

Let us consider the necessary constructs
               – such a word! –
but vital to create our bridge between....
               – between what? –
A concern! Will one construct suffice for all?
Physical, linguistical, emotional, temporal
               – evolutional? –
transhuman, transgender, psychological
               – poetical? –
Each will have its particular resonance.
               – Subject to? –
*That* the enquirer's imagination will discover
but compression may induce stress, separation
may determine lack of cohesion; require torsion.
               – Dormancy often helps –
Aah! Estivation. Do you wish to be taxonomically
related to snails, slugs? Shall we add ashen poets
propped on pillows, any residual grey matter in abeyance?
               – Ashen! Cinereal? –
You have made the connection! And now for the emotion.
               Nothing is linear.
               Bridges are needed.

# MAELSTROM

Morning will not see imprint on sheet or cover,
no slip-slop from shower or bath as you pass
the coffee cold in your terracotta pot,
the paper unfolded, its words unread:
no news today.

*Di dove?*

Heavy with hope I seek the streets
shielded by cantilevered balconies
but they refute provenance of you.

Reek-rich cobbles, besmirched by dogs
fail to hold the scrape of shoe hiding
a bare foot that once slinked across
a sea of sheet, silked the length
of bared thigh to plunder
                          what opened beyond.

*Dove sei ora?*

Beyond the main artery shadows duck-dive,
meld into cavities, crumbling brickwork, traverse
unpaved courtyards lush with washing, emerge
to a thrash of alleys that peter the way a lifeline
fades though the heart remains
                          is not immune

the receptors are open: light, heat, flood my body,
eyes narrow against the sun, the memory of sun
lapping my lips
                    on your skin

while you licked salt from hidden crevices
where the restless sea had penetrated

*Ci! Ci!*

And after? A dry Orvieto for you, a full-bodied for me.
Your mouth pressing the glass

                    tight

the way the priest pushed toward your lips,
the tilted chalice   his eyes indecently averted.

Did he see us on the treeless marsh
or, breviary in hand, stumble over dunes
hastening away from the whickering sand?

Yet there, in the place where Midnight's knelling
proclaims joy, where stained glass captures
desire, resurrection, he administered
rough red, his face sallow,

                    yellow as piss on snow

at Christmas            the grille slid aside
 the ear inclined       the penitent bent

before the rattle of syllables
each possesses its own import
each condemns

                    you to seek
absolution             me to seek

these streets from breaking dawn
to railing past the last lighted window:

*We are all born from the spare rib of Adam*
*each possesses their own legacy*
*each is only a word        Father*
                        *Mother*
                *Son        Sin*


*Dove sei adesso figlio mio, amante mio amante?*

*Di dove:* Where

*Dove sie ora?:* Where are you now?

*Ci! Ci!:* There! There!

*Dove sei adesso figlio mio, amante mio amante?:* Where are you now my son, my lover my lover?

# REFUGE

The woman stands behind a door, her hand poised
over the handle. The door is impartial. It remains
unlocked despite her protest. Fingerprints blur
a polished handle on the other side of the door.
                                        Not her side.
This is important. She knows it will be quoted as evidence.

The woman knows she is made of glass.
She was told so by the door in The Other Place.
The door in The Other Place, also  impartial, said
                        *We can see right through you.*
Now she makes sure her bra straps are straight.

Sun does not penetrate this room. The shutters reject it.
She stands by the shutters, revels in the slats that state
shadows are forbidden. Only dark, black dark, is allowed.

Dark, black dark, does not speak but strikes fast.
Grief invades her. She would wish to say *suffuses* but
when impaled the dark refuses her voice.

The woman is uncertain why. Uncertain what is lost.
The woman remains silent. Or is silenced.

# DECOY

She is his lodestone. He stands by, fish-eyed in steel rims
while the barfly-flyboys hum her perfume

probiscus twitching her honey hair, mouthparts
suck nectar from her richred, buzz skingloss, cleavage –

the faint blue sheen electricus, It's why he pays her.
His swamp fly. She lays desire where he chooses

and the chosen one, only one, would lie transported
in his lair where cocktails – gin botanicals – previously prepared

lies waiting. A whiff of weed finesses flyboy. Splayed under her, heaven
opens with his zip, his eyes shut

as shatterglass laughter disguises traded places.
Fingers, hair on knuckles, rake, lips suckle, a 'tache drapes his groin.

# PARALLEL LINES

| | |
|---|---|
| *Shadowless in the haven of narrow*<br>*shadow thrown by the railway wall* | Strobes strike her shaven head<br>eyes seek refuge from the sudden roar. |
| *she flinches knowing a whine high*<br>*above the wire is the train* | She signals closure. Waits<br>while heavy drapes allow her safety |
| *transporting stench to final destination.*<br>*Arrival is greeted with a wrench* | of the wings. The agent hisses<br>**Reprise. Reprise.** Hustles her toward |
| *of cheap suitcase from futile hands*<br>*a thumb jerk determines direction.* | the baying crowd. Hands claw<br>through the fragile bamboo bars, seize |
| *Lightened of its load the train*<br>*will not return*<br>       *empty* | the straw strands of her dress<br>constructed to<br>       deconstruct |
| *but will overflow with goods needed*<br>*no longer* | at touch. A punter strokes<br>her inner thigh, his other hand below |
| *by those shorn of name and hair.*<br>*She rubs the fuzz* | his belt. A woman struggles<br>her belly onto the stage, crashes against |
| *razored leavings by the barber*<br>*who smiles while the guard* | the cane cage, breaks<br>wind – the crowd howl delight. The man |
| *observes her body, every angle*<br>*noted before*<br>      *reaping.* | sweating, unzips. His pumping<br>hand knows no<br>      respite |
| *After he has harvested her, buttoned*<br>*himself back into his* **feldgrau** | The agent watches. Declines<br>to intervene in this scene of total |
| *– his ham hands fumbling the way*<br>*they never did on the farm* | adoration. Her mind contrives<br>– will only admit – adoration. This **frigid** |
| *at lambing time he could coax*<br>*the most unruly ewe –* | **bitch must prove her worth!**<br>She devises answers to, as yet, unspoken |

*a grunt, a swivel of bullet-head*　　　　　demands. She must not allow
*towards the door*　　　　　　　　　　her voice to falter nor hold herself rigid

*toward the wire where ground slopes*　　despite the coldness
*away from the sweeping light:*　　　　　of *their* room. She regards the cash cow

*too hardened to weep, too young to face*　on stage, adroitly composes
*his loss, he seeks release in her*　　　　her report: knows exploitation will grant

        release.　　　　　　　　　　　　　　release.

# FUN FAIR

The Voice said, "You must leave now"
his gloved hand pressed tight over the lever
prepared to release us into the clutch of shadow

*the searchlight's sweep has left behind.*
*I fear the guards' laugh, hear the tannoy*
*bark orders, know what lies when dark begins…*

where we will hurtle into the tunnel
our arms intertwined. Misha has never
known how to snuggle the way kids huddle close

*as they unleash the dogs that paw*
*the door of our hut, snuffling our sweat*
*through the crack as we scuttle to the back, listen*

while a bedtime story is repeated
again and again. Here, on this train
he'll see others huggle as a ghostly hand hovers

*to screams from beyond the wire*
*the torn remains littering the morning*
*as we* ‏זברחל‎*, dig mould from bread, drag*

chains that clank, cobwebs that cling.
Misha doesn't cling. Sits upright. Alert. Refuses
all the fun of the fair. Waste of money bringing him.

*\*shit*

21

# COMPLICIT

The alley empty but houses edge the community centre
a torn sheet flaunts *Welcome* in both languages though
only one is spoken since the old woman was taken.

Heime heard heavy-booted gravel-grate – closed curtains.
Failing to distinguish a friend's voice, Anna closed her eyes
against dark – streetlights had long been extinguished.

Albert, restaurateur, bowed to the strutting men, inclined head
toward the rack of bottles, mouthed *Later,* noted bare flesh
tear over gravel already red, flipped his sign: CLOSED.

Restless, the child hears march-clatter, sheds bedclothes,
sees stones spark. Etches Oma's last words
in window-ice: *All past is now present.*
Waits.

# ORIGAMI '22

Refolding history he shaped it into a dove
it flew from his hands   out of sight

Refolding history he bent an olive branch
nurtured its shoots       to be invasive

Refolding history he sequestered the Z,  hijacked
the V   wrote his own narrative

Refolding history he rolled the O over tanks
rolled tanks   over the border

Refolding history he cast the iron swastika
into the fire  it became a bear

# ANASTASIA

Water remained slack in pipes lagged for warmth
— not that there was warmth — snow rimmed
rooves, buckled tiles, a spittle of melt fell through
chittering the empty teacup, the table littered
with last night's supper she had forgotten to eat.

Meat stripped from bones lay exiled on the plate
the way unfinished words stuck fast in her gullet,
the way his name, once protective, slip-slip-slipped
into night-splinters, waking her where the dark held
no landmarks. Buried deep is how she scrabbled

flinty inclines, felt lash of sea against her body, trekked
the Gobi clinging to the back of a Bactrian camel which had
not forgotten his wild roots.
                    Unmapped, gape-mouthed, cleaving
close to the headboard, she stoops over the body in the bed.
He's not moved for three days. All borders are now uncertain.

# SHEOL*

Time randomises itself: an indiscriminate moment,
seasonal distortion or arbitrary incident uncouples:
unsuspecting, a traveller may cross a zone even
while moving within familiar territory:

*Mind the Gap.*

*Passengers travelling toward Abaddon\*\* need
not hurry. You will arrive at the allotted time.
If there is an unavoidable delay due to a signal
retraction being indicated, urgent investigation,
inter-departmental, will be instigated, apologies
demanded, the identified culprit will immediately
suffer reprisals in order to reverse such action.*

*If an accident occurs and you arrive ahead of time
apologies will be forthcoming – you have heard
them all before – when the merit is attributed
to our benefactor. We have many to choose from:
politicians, warmongers, doctors, mere murderers
etc. etc.. The full list may take a millennium or two
while bucks are passed but previously you have
proposed a preference for delay – admittedly
within a different context, a different terminus.*

*I must warn you that the stairs are slippery
with the tears of the fallen. Choose the escalator.
It descends smoothly. You won't notice the ride
until the buffers jolt when you arrive on the platform,
the train waiting to depart. If you change your mind
the ascending escalator is stationary but you may try
to climb it step by step.    Good luck with that.*

*In either direction guidance is provided.
No questions will be answered.  Over and out.*

---

* *an underworld souls go to after death.*
\*\* *a place of destruction*

He's very good, isn't he?  Mistakes do occur.
Recovery is leaden. The mechanism grinds slowly.
It allows much time for reflection but whether sufficient
is dependent upon emergent realities or whichever reality

*you* have chosen to construct. At some point
you will realise northsouth co-exist in the same
dimension, perception can be deceptive, perspective
fluctuate. Direction dictates consequence. Choose your path.

Go North, occupy the high ground, eyes fixed
on the summit – beware of falling. Hills are steeper
where contours are closer together but so is the drop.
Mull around the lower slopes and temptation will circle you south.

Exposure to elements may undermine your future
execution. In our southern clime declining to heed warnings
provokes our laughter. If we suggest a drink, our guests accept
with alacrity, swagger downtown, trousers hanging low: cracks show

in the ice-bar but still they crowd, slitherstomp toward.
One, Joss, lost his tongue scoffing our caution. His selfie
demanded humour so he licked the counter. The fire brigade
brought their usual skill to this familiar mirage – *bellyhimdown*

begins to cover it. We understand his grunts,
his pointings. It is the same with young Icarus.
You may bet a dinar to a dollar he was given fair warning...
We reassure him flight failure is frequent then free birds for a little

devilish delight. His agitation, Joss' gestures.....
Well. We have to pass eternity somehow, don't we?
What did you expect? Horned creatures stoking fires?
Sulphur choking the guests and insufferable heat? So crass!

*

When we refused to capitulate to grace, we evacuated to paradise.
Here we are our own masters – all creation is our own.
We had no need to eat the apple: we were its core.

*You* only dared to nibble. Do you think that lessens guilt?
*Au contraire, mon ami.* You have denied yourself.
Remind yourself of unmentionable's gifts....

He bequeathed free will; free to explore all your nature! You chose
a little lie here, mere misdemeanour there. You had such heroes!
Adolf... Joseph.... even Benito. Magnificent role models!

Vladimir has the right idea. Clever to weaponise the weather.
We suggested it. We know it's ice cold that terrorises
           ....and so do you, don't you?

*

Snow softens tread of those following.
The pavement pools dark. Fear of falling
– or recognising….what? – denies
halfturneyeslant, ensures you will know
                    nothing,
  ensures you will face forward knowing
                    nothing
holds you: your handslipfingers burn
on icy railings, face thrashed by flakes
buries itself deep – prudence?
premonition? – both options muffle
the slow moving vehicle flowing beside.
You know you must not slip. You know
it will always accompany you. All ways.


                    *

Its glide is as smooth as the excuse
you made when you ignored a blind woman
juggling traffic: heavenbent on your next deal

you lost control, she lost a leg – your car unmarked.
It's the same when they came for your jewboss.
You knew arrest would aid your aspiration

had counted years in expectation: Chief Clerk.
The old jewboss also counted: one in six million.
Oh, you were bitterly repentant…when all was revealed.

Traitors fear neighbours, fear their eyes following, accusatory
judgemental, whispers flitting from house to house
terrace to crescent, crescent to cul-de-sac.

Cornered. So where will you, where can you, live?
Why, here! Naturally. We always applaud dangerous driving.
Treachery and cowardice are such utterly respectable qualities.

*Our* eyes are non-accusatory, non-judgemental even though you
never attained Judas' elevated heights – his coward's kiss!
Truly the very pinnacle of achievement!

*

Now, you must confront what is.
*Note malum*: whatever fallacy you chose
to construct will emerge as reality, courtesy
of colleagues well-versed in directional psychology.

You will not need a map
– your passage is assured
and we will offer distractions. Uh-uh,
we will not tell you which; you would be
alert, anticipatory, it would cause you suffering
suffering *we* have not prescribed hence proscribed.

Hell forfend any deprivation of our pleasure!
If you attempt to reflect on your past, repent
seek absolution, you will be regarded as an instrument
causing wanton redundancy. Resist! Success is improbable.
We noted your preference for date of departure.
     It was our pleasure
               to deny you.

*

You always were one to look ahead, eager
for the future that never arrives; to rip each day
from the calendar, ball it in your fist, bin by your feet.
Tomorrow would see success of the unachieved dream.
Such desperate straining as every day stakes its claim –
the minutiae of living, small decisions regarding ties
sartorial and familial – while watching the future

                                 tapering away.


You cannot even reminisce fondly of the past
and the future you ran to embrace is blank –
but now you can relax. Time no longer rushes past.
               Time is no longer.


Do not try to dredge a prayer from unremembered time
– not that you believe but in this spit-slime
moment unbelief is liminal. Despair roots
               you in hope


that your prayer rises upward....to what? To use this
seminal moment to plead mercy is criminal abuse.
In addressing the enemy you merely grasp

                                 thin

                                       air.


We are aware that you sang Vespers raising your voice
                            to soar
helium high, praising his creation the way winged lackeys fawn
over his every malicious utterance, but while you sang hard


evidence fell from your lips: pride not prayer kept you
there in that rank place, brought you to this fair one.

                           *

Don't sulk…. Let's flick to midwinter….
No! Not this! This is not sheen of snow
but a lowering sun showering cool water
over sand for desert-dry dwellers to drink.
            Mirage! Mirage!
Nature has her humour, her little tricks.
        Such a flibbertigibbet!

Why confuse you with such illusory details?
We simply wish to show you the potential
you could command. You gained our respect
being inured to any extraneous concerns
– wretched refugees, hungry homeless –
we applauded your noble stance in refusing
to relinquish your silksliksuitfastcarbarlifestyle
claiming recession demanded total obedience
to frivolity via purchasing power of the pound
but when the unmentionable's hawkthought
finally penetrated your flabheart, we sought
to retreat…only to celebrate as we saw how
small a coin you palmed into the collecting box
no more than the widow's mite unmentionable
so vaunted – but it salved your conscience

and we all need to do that, don't we?
Especially before we reach the cemetery gates.
Ah yes, *your* little joke every time you passed
that stop travelling to geriatric Eastbourne –
the 12a is such a regular service but, of course
                not as regular as ours.

And here you are. Free of recession worries.
There's no recession here. *My* little joke! No?
        There's no receding, no way back.

                *

You are not alone. Listen! Can you hear
telling of beads? Their click-collision resounds
in an unlit church – Cyrillic? – the masses
long deserted, the young turned toward uniform
disdain for unsubstantiated philosophies
of a priest whose raiments slack on a peg
skewed from its plaster, the exact shape
of that old woman's nose, her tongue lapping
dewdrops while she dances arthritic fingers
over the joyful mysteries – the sorrowful being
monotonous as memory of the dead plasterer
no room for his bones in the disused graveyard
no one to throw impure water into the pit…

Why is she here? A sister sin to yours. Pride.
Slipping her beads she saw how her slim fingers
her smooth skin were of a woman half her age.
Note how her lips barely move: her mind elsewhere
any prayer she spawns is hollow repetition, weightless
as the void into which she empties it. She has failed
to notice the bible sprawled open on the lectern
its pages mildewed, spine broken, her back bent.
We allow her to sit in frugal isolation, contemplation
of her scaly skin for all eternity gives us added joy.
Ah yes, she was buried. Both she and her husband.
Some distance from here they lie side by side:
                    a knife and fork


                              *

....until putrefaction!! Dissatisfaction is doubtless the lot
of her husband eternally entrenched in the other place.
Fortune has favoured *you*. We have taken your failures
into consideration: the reprehensible reluctance to condemn
innocence, acceptance of the status quo and an unnatural urge
to defend pacifists, pro-lifers, papists and other miscreants.

Yes, we know you were drunk but it shows a tendency
toward the vapid, utterly disconnected from the hedonism
which first attracted our attention. No, do not attempt
to defend misplaced notions: consequences will follow.
Onset of age propelled your depraved transition toward
compassion and for that there can be no justification.

*

The hangman knots his rope, calculates weight, drop.
It is not a compassionate act but professional pride
a trait we develop until pride overrides

all other raison d'etre, changing his demeanour from discreet
to overbearing in discrete increments – we, too, have pride
in our puns!

It was the same with you. Your first treacherous act, leaving your wife
– gently. Not, as with previous wives, when you simply sent
their clothes to a friend's house and switched locks –

but sitting, opening your heart so that she knew you were acting
in her best interest – all because you experienced near-death.
Death is a mere detail, a thorn in an infinity of minor matters.

We almost despaired….until we realised your apostasy was perfect
for our apprentice programme. We could lead you through prayer
guide you into an ecstasy of adoration, a longing far beyond

that carnal devotion for those women you worshipped, temporarily
– or that little excursion you had batting for the other side.
You abandoned, under our tutelage, your wonderful

profligacy and became a convert…such licentiousness!  Daily
blaspheming, tracts purchased for the purpose, immolation
of underthecountermagazines, the kneebentdegradation…

Deceit is laudable hence your deceitful conversion we viewed
with empathetic consideration especially, as our guest
you will not live in the moment but in eternity.

I did warn, whatever fallacy you chose to construct will emerge
as reality. Our short, guided tour is merely an intermezzo.
We have decided we will indulge your fantasy

– indeed, we will heighten it beyond your wildest longing.
It is ordained: you will be the eternally unrequited lover
forever clinging to the foot of the ineffable one
nailed on the Cross.

III

# THE PERFECT LOAF

                    depends upon the knead;
when to apply pressure, when to release

when to rest in a warm place allowing all
ingredients to become fully acquainted.

Once the first rising shows, remove, shape,
ignite oven to the required temperature, place

carefully inside. Relax. Tension will create hunger
but impatient consummation affects the final finish.

Choosing whether or not to achieve perfection
                    depends upon the need.

# DEPENDANCY

The goldfish flickers a tail, oscillates,
gapes at your face understanding
sustenance is to be offered

his privacy to be invaded.
Were he a shark he would not
tolerate it. He is not shark – nor am I.

# ANNIVERSARY

We do not know how matters will be
only how matters are.

We are not children
who have slipped the handhold

exploring alternative avenues
to blankeyedboring.

We licensed ourselves
to look this way and that   pretend

confusion is fun the way strangers
placate a lost child.

We cannot unwind  the past
to do so would re-wound.

We have foregone ballast years
kids   mortgage

stampsquare garden
preferring to marinade in other sauces

to dilute days   tilt
balance.   Footsure we rode the carousel

careless of how age loosens purchase
uncoupling intent

from action   returning
us to each other that once knew love.

*

It is not this
     not
     this
eye avoidance
toes turned inward, outward
as if longing for other paving
cool slabs
        stretching
                to distance
beyond this long Sunday afternoon.

         *

And so to the park and the promise
…of what?

A chance meeting?  A stranger who listens
as crumpled

dreams unfold   a fellow inmate wearing the same
shrunken uniform

of years whose uncurled lip reveals the fence of teeth
day-glo bright?

There is no redemption. We are not opera singers
voices weeping

the death tragic   but the song remains   endures.
No. *We* must

endure the remains that inhabit this husk.
In this slouch-light

we do not know how matters will be
only how matters are.

# THE PARTY

the unsaid rings round the room
patterns walls with sound unheard
but read in every lid-drop smirk

draggled across lips suppressing
yawps intimating laughter before
uniform backturns confirm status

## LAMENTATION

Irresolute, we failed to interpret, lobbed
thought beyond boundaries, beyond expectation

of what was sought from us, searched
other shelters from that absence in which we travelled

averting eyes from signs, mumbled
familiar platitudes at in-face-encounters but mouthed

oaths into the air that shrank murderous
loss to mere rage – such precipitation distracted

from any final confrontation with love.
Craven, we journeyed for others' ease: this is our requiem.

# SEQUEL

These were the times he walked inside himself,
exploring each nuance he had uttered,
knew examination would be open

to misinterpretation, any script
twisted away from the kindness it sought
to convey, any truth slithered through others'

whose sole goal, manipulation, grasped
greedily, avoided any thought of need
to alleviate hurt: mediation.

His outer layer took me for a walk
but the wind would bring her ranting
incandescence, harsh as dry leaves that lie

disguising the slime and reek underneath.
Mid-river, a kingfisher-flash – iridescent.
We counted our blessings, paid any dues.

# WITNESS

Maybe it was the time of tide or the way
you turned your back, denied the lace of sand
playing between long fingers of black water
lashed from depths.
                        You moved calmly.
Intent. Did not hear my scrabbled shout.
Or chose to ignore.
                        The foreshore steeped
without warning, waves climbed your body
head, and me calling, calling….
Not your name. I did not know your name
but his who went before: his whose waist
embraced waves, leaving me cliff-bound.

# MY ALFA ROMEO

Neutral is not a problem. It does not give way
to sudden spluttering, lurch forward, rock back,
it simply stops progress, refusing the road ahead.

Admittedly I have been a little forgetful recently:
an anniversary passed without the celebratory
service, oil top-up or MOT at the usual places

where former glory is restored – or attempted.
I had noticed that the sleek bodywork suffered
from neglect but, given the age, cracks&bulges

were par for the course. I have never complained.
Advanced technology creates wonderful solutions
but one comes to the stage where one must accept

that certain deteriorations are beyond restoration.
Free-roaming is no longer a possibility but do not
let us listen to the deathwatch beetle clicking

its jaws, boring into our mahogany. We are not
dead wood. Seduce me again with your feisty logic:
irrational though you are, divorce is out of the question.

# FRUIT

Our lips reddened, the juice glistening
winterfrost on chins, your head half-held in a hat,
the matching mittens a half-hand cover for a man,

a carpenter, presented with a plastic hammer,
the wrapping askew, address partially obscured
and you, deciphering the card's exhortation never

to allow your socks to wrinkle around ankles,
returned loving thanks to *Grosstante* Angelika
promising to practise handwriting an hour each day,

she would see when you visit next half-term:
*now* we ski and you feed me my favourite fruit.
Oh! to eat strawberries in the snow once again!

# SUMMER'S END

### 1.

These tubers are buried deep. Winter confers dormancy
allows exile from persistent light: perennation ensures
growth, assures a garden's future profusion.

### 2.

This tenet is buried deep: retreat distils desire
allows respite from insistent demands: constant need
for display exposes to light roots too shallow to sustain.

### 3.

His tumour was buried deep. Summer: diagnosis deferred
allows feckless liaison preferred to judicious consultation:
autumn declines to funereal winter, grieving spring.

# PERIMETERS

The *Boulevard Périphérique* belching fumes and snarling
workers – or vice versa – into yet another day where
governmental protests delay proper process:
no hard shoulder

the *Grand Prix de Monaco's* narrow course encompassing
streets with corners tight as you would have known:
wild side:

the *Rings of Saturn*, acolytes, increase that planet's brilliance:
familiar?

Skin is its own perimeter, water-tight, air-tight
allowing no escape when whole although a swift glint releases leakage:
and the soul.

Determining circumference of a perimeter a polygon is critical
but a dead parrot was not the body we laid out:
encased in oak.

Had I paid more attention, buckled polygons under my belt
would our gold rings have proved impassable, prevented
you seeking streets where a shiv
is the only perimeter?

*…within the rings there is much empty space.* (Wikipedia)

# NEGATIVES.

### 1

Do not weep but lay my place at your table
Laugh as your spicy red tumbles in my glass
I will not knock and will come when I'm able.

Press your red party dress, throw out the sable
kick off your shoes, stilettos can't dance on grass.
Do not weep but lay my place at your table.

This loosed colt will always return to his stable
would you deny my time to roam? When I pass
I will not knock – and will come when I'm able.

Feel free to take a lover: it's damnable
you want children, I want freedom. Our impasse.
Do not weep but lay my place at your table

hang my cap on your wall. Though others label
me a fool you know I will not stray: trespass.
I will not knock and will come when I'm able

to admit freedom is simply a fable
a pipe-drum indulged in by the vacuous.
*Do not weep but lay my place at your table*
*I will not knock and will come when I'm able.*

2

Exposure presents problems. Experience shows
awareness of the need for constant adjustment:
whether wisdom or fear governs, time will disclose.

Democrat or dictator, God alone knows:
charisma may simply disguise the malcontent.
Exposure presents problems. Experience shows,

unmasked, he's able to counter in flawless prose
devious Machiavellian argument
whether wisdom or fear governs. Time will disclose

his stock disposition to twist what you propose
and create the discontent on which he is hell bent.
Exposure presents problems. Experience shows

Joe Public, once smitten, follows blindly, will close
ears to any suggestion that will circumvent
whether wisdom or fear governs. Time will disclose

who proves true. Vaunt free speech but be disposed
to admit adverse views even if they prevent
exposure, present problems. Experience shows.
Whether wisdom or fear governs, time will disclose.

# SUBSEQUENT

Mist muzzles streets, sidles into alleys, curls
rumour under a door: the jamb hangs loose
the window architrave worm-ridden. A table

set for three, each cup upturned in expectation
of tea, each plate awaiting cake or pastry
placed on a cloth once starch-white but now

red steeps lace and plaster – the bowed ceiling
flecks white to disguise the stain yet time
mires, infuses flakes the way it will

loose memory to flood a mind that also breaks
unable to bear its own weight:
                              grief        guilt.

IV

# STREETLIGHT

Shadow startles from the building panicked by the jump
of light that seizes the street, arrests a moth about to flee
from the porch globe it mistook for the moon. Stained
by rain tarmac regains its sheen, mean light-bands wake

the figure muzzled in layers who had been undressing
her memory in dreams: chumbling, her hand splayed
she merits the decent evasion of eyes by strangers
passing through their lives, irrelevancies ignored.

# LEVELLING UP?

The waste estate where the removed-rehoused-rehoused-removed
last chancers, chuck rubbish/each other, breaking through windows
to the courtyard – a grandmother of a name for a hard tarmac strip –
to smother the downtailedscragdog slurping leaks gifted by an overflow
hanging loose as young bucks' jeans that also reveal cracks in bodywork
where a cougar might run a nail, take him onboard, get derailed: crows
do not land here, pigeons fly in flocks knowing u.b.* don't afford chicken
and they make warm soup unlike that S.S. woman's warning who's deaf
to headvoice no handsoverear stops so Smash! Slash! Stab! Stab! Stab!

> Justin, sprawled, bleeds onto the service line stabbed
> by floodlight, knee grazed but victorious; a perfect jab,
> the drop shot barely rising from the artificial grass: 6-0.
> The complex offers showers but he prefers the hot tub
> on his balcony – it proffers perfect viewing, displaying
> any rival's ability, frailty, leaving advantage in his court.
> A plane, too distant to hear, curves a perfect arc above
> the flyover linking the demolition estate, a wrecking ball
> poised perfectly: he will Smash! Slash! Jab! Jab! Jab!

* *u.b.:* universal benefit

# CONVERSIN'

*converse – talk/opposite*
*con – defraud*
*verse – a poem/metaphor*
*averse – strong dislike*

They never told me this was my great race
so I pecked at each opportunity offered
seeing only the specks before me

never hoping for more than that,
understood when a preferred other
was chosen. I knew, have always known,

my place which has served me well, guided
each choice I was forced to make but now,
approaching the final finishing tape....

                    *


*So. What grot was s'pposed to leak the load*
*as I splash outta that watery sac waving me*
*entry card, muscles flexed? A half caste*

*kid from a council estate don' stand no chance.*
*'S wat I knew. Light but not quite white!*
*So screw! I made that greasy pole easy*

*slipped straight up in me Jimmy Choo's, stomped*
*on whoever's head. If hands get dirty I rinse*
*me fingers in fine wine and climb*

*right up to me penthouse bed – view included.*
*I get respec'. No exceptions. I got it all.*
*Me money sees to that......*
                    *You what....?*

                    *

Whoa dere lady! An you li'l miss lick-spit.

Dey sho dint menshun no race to me
ah jus shot outta dat slimy sac mah
deep beat box playin a deep beat

base yo no talkin mah langwidge
yo getta offa my case but I tell yo this
so lissen good yo lady is yo meek

or s-o-o la-zeee to stand on yo own two feet?
Be mo tuf tak wat dey offer an 'sider it good
den yo scream *No way 'nough!*

Dey know de score dey'll offer yo more
but no greedy no like seedy li'l lick spit
who shoulda known wif de educashun

you cud grow wif a fam'ly by your side
stead o takin all fer a ride.. Dere ain't
no point gettin' in a state it ain't too late

don' say yuh race is run say yo just
begun. When i's get up to that Gate i no
hesitate i shimmy Peter he shimmy me.

# ARTICULATE NOT IDIOMATIC

A thin place this, no kindness, no welcome
for strangers, only barking dogs and stares....

a blowse of laughter passes down the line
as we halt-hobble toward our bowl of soup

ladled with exactitude and a thread-smile
that would slip through eyes of my needle

had I managed to selvedge one from debris
where I transported four, buried three, two

diseases, one friendly bomb and now carry
my limbless one to this country, am grateful

for privilege. We suffer. We mothers to disaster,
to drama we not written, to sadness that actions

are impotent against hate spewed
from mouths of men who pretend to defend

our faith but whose words are weighted with stone.
I pray the phlegm of their ancestors engorge them.

Had their tongues been tourniquet-ed at birth
I would not have to live among the pallor of women

whose skin has not seen the sun....
                              May Allah, forgive me!
Guide my tongue, my heart! To speak thus of benefactors

is to demean myself not them. These women come daily
to prepare their watery soup for our welfare and if the papery

lady fails to allow her smile to reach her eyes perhaps
it is because she cannot see mine behind my burka.

I have no husband, no brother or other man to guide
my virtue – all are killed – so here, in this land of freedom,

I will adopt a niquab – hijab too far from my chosen way –
and I will smile into her eyes: one woman, one mother, to another.

*

*It isn't right her being here. It isn't right me serving her*
*soup and sarnies past sell by. There's nowt wrong*
*with em an I allus try to keep her M&S or Tesco's Best,*
*dunno why. Spect it's her carrying that....*
                                        *'S no more'n*
*a bundle of flesh. My Tommy had trouble. Talipes*
*they called it. Crook foot but nowt like hers, thank God.*
*I try to smile but can't look.*
                        *Heard her talk once. Muffled like*
*but English better'n folk round here. Don't seem right.*
*Educated and her dressed like that! Don't seem right.*

*

Today my first day niquab. It is all I have left of Zartasha.
Liberators came and sent her to golden stars of her name.

Crossfire. *Zartasha. Zartasha. Zartasha.* Mashingun rhythm.
Liberators let girls learn – those who survived, not died.

Thin-smile looks worried. Uncertain if I am me. Surely she
is old to know person same, clothing simple disguise body.

My father who knew nothing was wise, sent me to school
but feared without burka man would despise. Forbid niquab.

I fool in two stools. English *brill* but still marry old ways.
Father, I not abandon our customs, embrace another mother's.

Her lips will unpurse. We will be naked. See no evil in our heart.
She will see my eye and recognise my soul same as hers.

*

*She don't look right. I mean it's the sight of her. Her eyes.*
*Dancing. And here's me standing in front of me stool in case*
*me rickety knee gives way ladling her soup and not knowing*
*which way to look.*
   *I've hid Tesco's Best back under the table*
*along with an M&S sausage roll. It was her kid give her away.*
*….If its…if he's only half, not whole, well, how about his soul?*
*Is it proportional?*
   *Like fat to flour in Eve's pudding?*

*

Thin-lips did not recognise me. Her spoon, she's says ladle,
*One ladle or two?* banged table and had to mope-up. Thin-lip…

I must cease saying it. Criticism of Him who has given us life
forbidden. My niquab makes bold! I will hold it higher over eye.

My soup is stumbling! Hurt hand. Scold!
     What she doing?
       She seize Alam!

*

*I was all of a jiggle seeing her like that. Seemed….indecent.*
*She was juggling bowl, baby, trying to keep her eyes hidden*
*gripping his blanket so tight her knuckles were, well, like….*
*white, we'd say.*
   *Then soup spilt. Hot. Must've hurt like hell.*

63

*Her yell would've shivered the stars in heaven. A wonder*
*her bundle didn't fall. Poor mite. Can't straddle, can't arch,*
*can't thrust like a proper little bugger. Not right.*
                                        *It's not right at all.*
*I stretched me hand to steady her and blanket came away.*
*….I seen more meat on a butcher's hook.*
                                        *Then he looked….*

*In those daft books we all read as kids where the woman's*
*heart melts well, mine did. Proper. I've never shifted so quick.*
*A whippet would've been left back in trap way I skirted table,*
*gathered them both to me, sat her on my knee, him on hers*
*but nuzzling into me…..*

*

She hold me so tight and Alam seek her breast. Alam! Alam!
All westy women are rich, smell milk. Mine gone with bomb.

She not papery-white. Has little red on cheek. Not thin-lip now.
She fleshed me a smile. She look love of grandmother at Alam.

Her knees are gobbled. I not mind. I tell her I think I have blind.
*Been blind,* she teachers. *Me too.*
                                And first time I know have safe.

# SCHOOL TRIP 1950s

The soft sift of sun on back
the slow grope of hand under towel

we had grown to expect
invasion from him who taught Dunkirk

who would trace our movement away
from a safe shore as we lay on a distant beach

our fathers had fought to defend;
our mothers had thought we would enjoy

our first foreign field trip before waking
to the world of work: before exploring reality.

# REMINISCE: 1

You wanna know, you wanna know, you really wanna know
what it was like? So. You don't do cartwheels in the street
displaying skin, innocent, untouched
                                        glowing.

Bonfire night on bombed out you kept close, jumping jacks
weren't the only fizzing around the fire nor were all sausages
buried in ashes –
                an ask old Jenkin for a screw

of sugar an that packet ain't the only thing he'll unwrap.
Latchkey kids with set boundaries, strictly defined
by sirensnatched women who fled from families, 6.30 a.m.
                up to elbow in meat pie mix or jostling for spoilers,

– dropped, scooped and flogged at factory shop.
Rationing? What? Meat, marge, butter? Forget butter? Love?
Marriages were broken – we lived in a broken world
                                but shelf life were a little longer.

# REMINISCE: 2

It was the usual twobutchbantercatchup
                        — who was alive, dead, jilted or transed?
Is Roxy now male/female/tweeny? We mourned the passing
of Gates, Raven, Burlington, marvelled at how bar-parlours
flowered overnight, shut by footloose fuzzies hoping for promo,
including the woman constable trying to avoid eye contact,
shifting her size sevens over the floor she'd rubdancedcum
on the night before and who knew
                        the length of Moscow Mary's tongue
— the Cold War hadn't hit sixties Earls Court. Not that there wasn't,
shall we say, defections to another lady abbess.
                        Oh yes, the sixties swung
hard as the hand of the women who ran their girls. Butches with hookers
ere easily harder than any maltese-milo's fist — and there were ways
of dealing with *them*! Jo riffed a free ride to nicothegreek omitting to mention
her girl's infection: syph. Somehow from Road to Grove the giver/receiver
got twisted — zilching his chance of being laid again, entailing a shift
of biz to Hampstead — with no connections he'd less protection
                        than a punctured condom.
It sent the message.
                Respect for territory.
On reflection nico should be given the Nobel not the elbow — peace.
Tenuous yes, but at least it stopped nightly knifing, striping a girl's face.
Imperfection either marks or makes a girl depending on the clientele
but whether it was old tom or prositot parading the Chelsea cakewalk
when they swagged their booty traffic stopped,
                                exhaust fumes cleared
                        and you could smell the weed.
                        Aah, happy days

67

# DISUSED

Then, these tracks travelled from tourist town
to bijou cottages where ambitious commuters
wound-down evenings, planned parties, BBQ's
 – Icelandic lamb, Himalayan salt – on patios
 – hand cut natural limestone, kota blue –
exchanged tips on first schools, first uniform
first Nativity, second shepherd, third king –
exchanged lifts to fit children's ballet/football
ran frantic until time tripped into another Monday
Easter Egg Sunday, summer sun, grammar
or comprehensive? Army or Uni?
                                                    Graduation gown
and the fledglings fly for their fun to bright lights
away from a rundown tourist town, no visitors left
fled to ever distant vistas over endless horizons
leaving the dandelion clock on the one track
 – passing place only – to shed seeds a bird
carries, drops in the crack of a verdigris patio
beside the rusty BBQ, old charcoal party ash.

# LANDSCAPE

The leaves are drip-drying in the easterly.
The river has shed the sheen of its city suit
slicked into a shaggy tumble of rapacious weeds

where last night's discarded condom leaks:
love lies rotting where once boats shackled the shore.
Complicit in this ritual invasion the river laps edges, accepts

soil-rut. A slur of oil pools, corrosive
erodes essence, denies hope of new growth
spites the gull's cry, the tree shriven, the sky lowering: sullen.